DRAWN

Peter Hughes is a poet and visual artist who is based in Umbria.

Also by Peter Hughes

Lent	(Equipage, 2024)
The Modulus of Rupture	(Shearsman, 2023)
Arrangements [with Eléna Rivera]	(Aquifer, 2022)
A Berlin Entrainment	(Shearsman, 2019)
via Leopardi 21	(Equipage, 2017)
Cavalcanty	(Carcanet, 2017)
Quite Frankly (Petrarch versions)	(Reality Street, 2015)
Allotment Architecture	(Reality Street, 2013)
Selected Poems	(Shearsman, 2013)
Interscriptions [with John Hall]	(KF&S, 2011)
The Pistol Tree Poems [with Simon Marsh]	(Shearsman, 2011)
The Summer of Agios Dimitrios	(Shearsman, 2009)
Nistanimera	(Shearsman, 2007)
Paul Klee's Diary	(Equipage, 1995)
The Metro Poems	(The Many Press, 1992)
Odes on St. Cecilia's Day	(Poetical Histories, 1990)

CONTENTS

ISBN: 978-1-917617-18-5

Cover designed by Aaron Kent

Edited by Andre Bagoo

Typeset by Aaron Kent

Broken Sleep Books Ltd
PO BOX 102
Llandysul
SA44 9BG

Drawn

Peter Hughes

Broken Sleep Books

FOR SIMON SMITH'S BIRTHDAY

I've always liked misreading you at dusk
& staring away from the wine cellar
as I call the fold-out cardboard storage pouffe
I got for four quid in Home Bargains
then rammed with Asda Pecorino plus some
Montepulciano from Bethesda or Abruzzo
& a couple of bottles of Spitfire
for example here you jog into the Hollywood
car-wash in a luminous cagoule
or there you go sat in the perfect A-line frock
with Metro polkadots rattling through Manhattan
or guiding a turret of love up La Manche
or wearing those tiny lights of raindrops that glisten
on your long black woollen coat & boots
on one of which a sparrow's feather clings
as you steam out of the rain into the pub
where we deconstructed cheese & onion
dereliction of one kind or another &
rueful smiles & sighs before the eyebrow
rises followed by the owner on his way back to the bar
near the rainy station or salt marsh or bookshop
or poetry reading venue-cum-morgue
good job there was a poetry revival
at this point my old friend you'll be aware
you can get a railcard up to two weeks
before your 60th birthday but cannot use it
until the day itself also buying online is easy
with a debit card & passport number

if you prefer to buy from a staffed station
you can use your birth certificate & poetry
to prove both your & age & identity
the latter liable – as Peter Riley pointed out –
to lurch in any direction away from pure Smithness
before winking & heading out the door

LET'S DANTZ

1

half way through a Leopardi rewrite
David Rees came to me in a vision
manning a mobile karaoke booth
that featured sparkling astral projections
of one Pan's person after another
in the lockdown lukewarm London night
I nearly spilt my tea in the abyss
& spasmed to a Françoise Hardy song
so I knew it was time to reload with
Stone's ginger wine & an Aldi speyside
single malt loaf pressed against each ear
then head along the path up through Braichmelyn
(which certain locals say is not called that)
emerge upon a gorse shelf in the sky

2

under the sign of the blue square halo
the river of death jogs on
I think it's in E ♭
most of the air we breathe is memory
a picnic & swim on Ynys Llanddwyn

a bit of Polish pork loin from Llandudno

over a flask of tea we remembered
Blake said trees were the imagination

& even in Venice
Canticles are not a breakfast cereal

like the small penguins of Tasmania
we've undergone a catastrophic moult

we're going home
we're dirty boppers

3

Talking Heads said she was moving into
the universe moving this way & that
& she was she was riding an NSU Quickly
down the Cowley Road at 4 in the morning
she was skating along the Brighton promenade
she was standing on the ferry cross the Mersey
she was changing trains at Gard du Nord
she was boarding Metro A at Anagnina
she was catching that San Giovanni tram
she was leaving from Schönefeld Airport
Dave's calling out for his telescopic de Kooning mop
& some of that krunchy nut yellow
he sometimes puts in people's eyes & lamps

4

I believe it was your man Corcoran
who introduced me to Caitlin Canty
who as it happens is performing now
in so far as that has any meaning
as we gingerly entered the dark halls
of the Covid & Rhubarb Triangle
as if it were the 700th time
our old red hats still bobbing in the gloaming
I love a bit of rustling in the morning
uncovering the long pink stalk before
it softens into nothing but its soul
O rosy & delicate translucent blob
chillin' in the porridge's warm dimple
Caitlin's singing get up get up get up

5

the venue resembled a Weatherspoons
collaged onto an Amazon warehouse
queues extending back as far as Dover
what with the self-imposed staff shortages
>   none of the punters still possessed a nose
>   having cut them off to spite their faces
>   into which they now decanted lager
>   washed down with lager for eternity
Transcendental Étude Opus fuck knows
the one where Puck & an entourage of
pissed Will-o'-the-Wisps trash the beach again
>   you still can't move for rancid troubadours
>   in rusty vans held together with Rizlas
>   playing anti-vax medleys on a tongue drum
Dave wipes something nasty off his Pan pipe
& pastes another nymph onto the night

6

in my dream I came out of a coma
or crystallised out of the national marsh
& Roberto Benigni was speaking
of all the directors he had worked with
& about his wife & about Dante
I dreamed we'd been dug out of the swamp
& stoop of contemporary Britain
& felt happy to be in this sculpted
valley of the beaver & butterwort
y tafod y gors - the tongue of the bog
I was thinking of aiming for heaven
but turned left at the end of Llyn Ogwen
& followed the course of Afon Lloer
up the southern slopes of the Carneddau
as far as its wide lap of resources
in Ffynnon Lloer - the Well of the Moon
you sense the stars inhabiting the lake
& I'm glad it can't be seen from the road

7

a vast origami fortune teller
now occupied the whole of the heavens
as I lay on my back on the hillside
surrounded by the local sheep & goats

this eery cootie catcher was adorned
with mystical symbols & equations
inexplicable signs & broken code
written out in gel pen & bright glitter

& in my waking vision I pointed
at a random or inspired selection
& watched as the flaps began to open

'you forgot to buy line for the strimmer'
'put this in your ear & set light to it'
the third said 'just press save & send to Dave'

SKODA

some of the Skoda's
in the ditch
as the wide black bird
flaps east so as not to slide
off the edges of evening
we tend to stay put
what with with the paperwork
& axe-storage issues
but keep our options open
as long as these prescriptions last
& most of the motorways
& airports remain open
the light is often one of those
1960s spirituals
that then turned into ads
for dreary beer & sweatshop jeans
so we go back to the Dutch guys
on the coast of Clare or Donegal
check on the Albanian painters of south Rome
& try to understand
their skills & dedication
we set off far too late towards Frascati
& its tendency to catch the light too early
Jarrett & the grape vine loop
possibly the Tokyo encore
nothing but everything
gets left behind
we seek to dodge the cause

of our own shadows
without the help of dove or raven
cut it back to just two shoots
the barrel getting lighter
more abstracted
less containing
less contained
first autumn morning &
the way September
& the lines turn into air

DRAWN
for Lisa Santana Hudson

1

Well of the Moon

& light blue
threads
still pulsing

underground

beneath the skin
& down the inclinations
of the catchment

on the rock wall
fresh sketches
of ancient constellations

& Orion
a reminder
of time's arrow

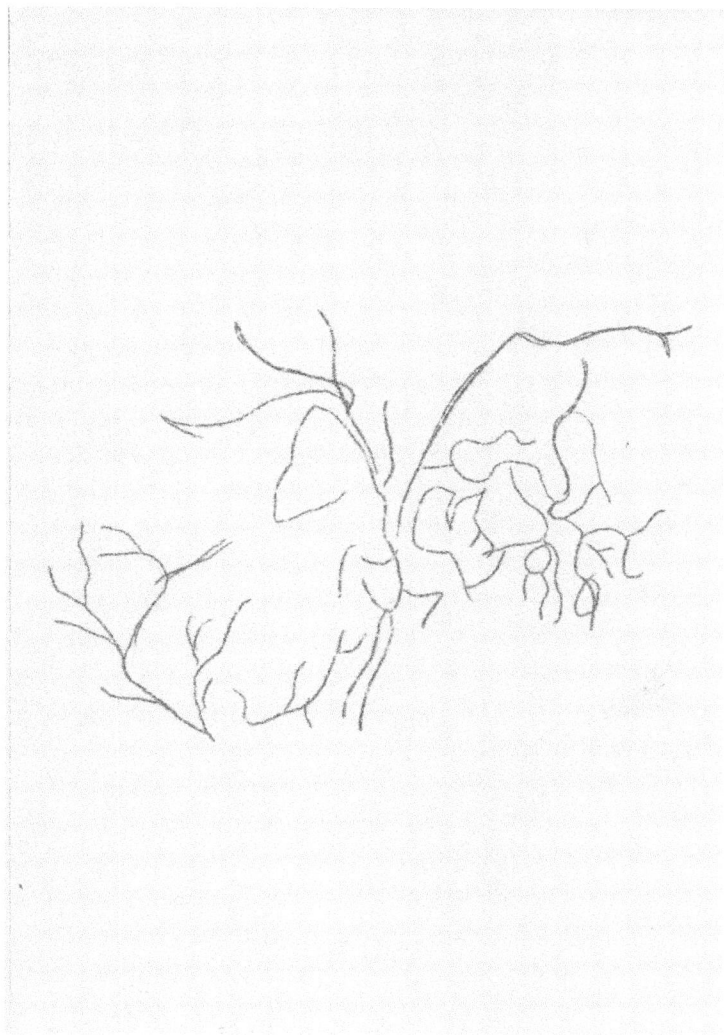

2

limbs flutter up through depths
in a new mobility of light

& white water under
& over rocks
pummelling the mad effusions
peat juice oxygen & tonic
& is it hunger

packhorse bridges

power lines through drifted
inconsistent mist

feathers of unhinged
life stream mountains rising
into rain then higher
to the west
glows & blues

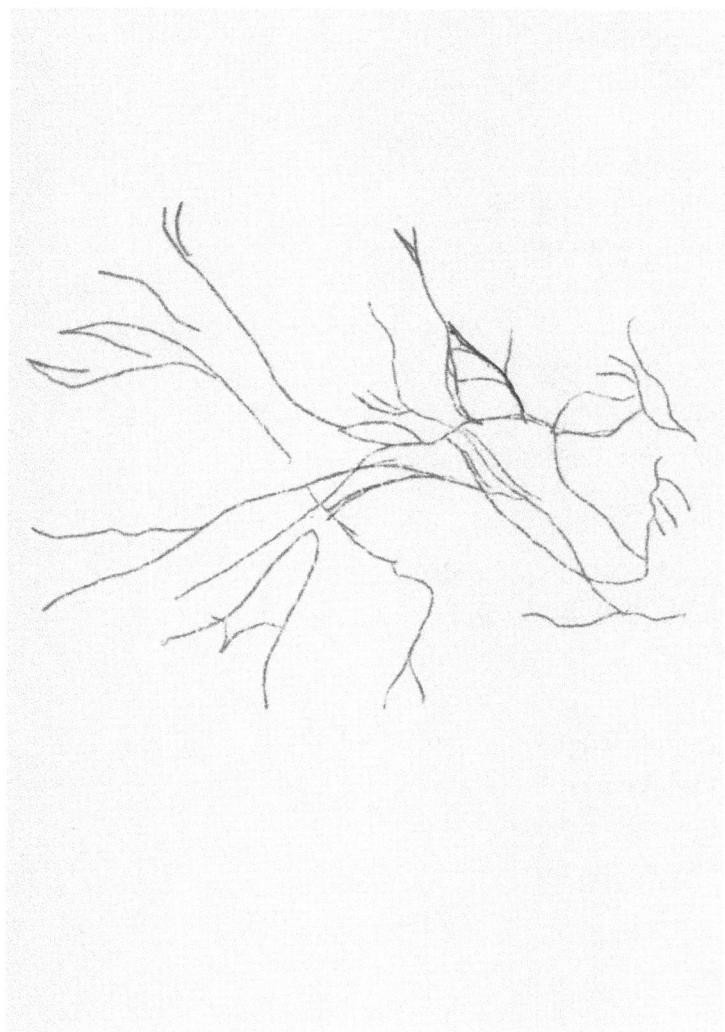

3

dusk silhouette
unexpected presence
at the gates of dereliction

kinks & fruiting
bodies of lost memories
dumped in the cart

time buffs
the small concavities
& protuberances
inhaling & exhaling
tracing

dotted lines & glyphs
the bridleways & footpaths
of the sensed & the imagined

returning to ovals
of exfoliation
frost on glass & then
that candle in the window

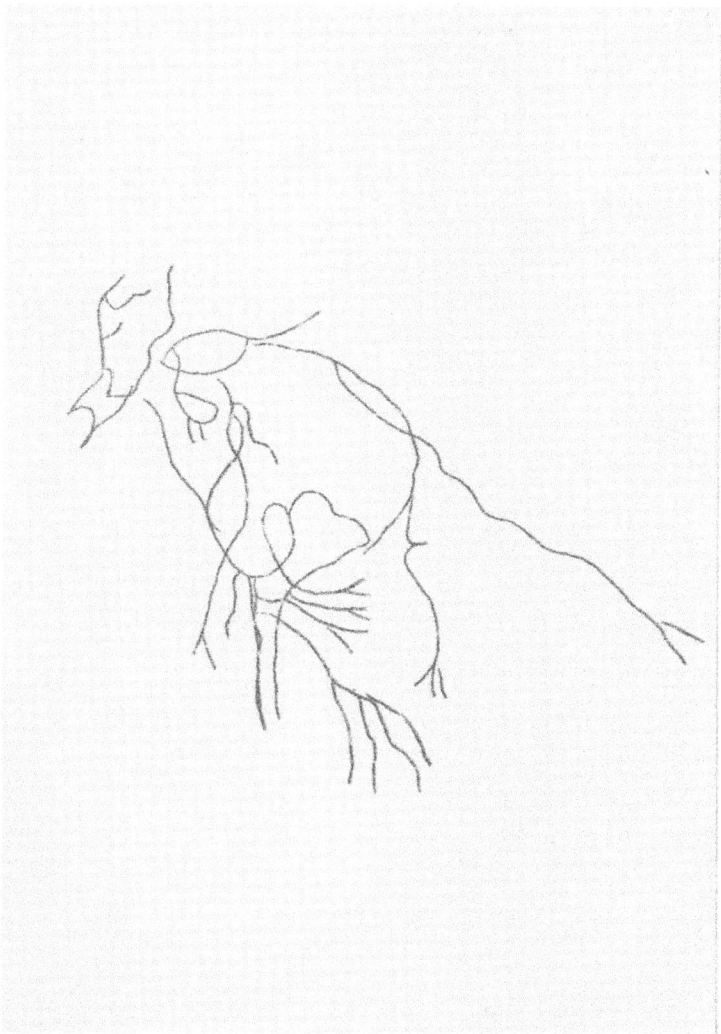

4

the last songs remain
the first heaved up the valley
to the starker shoulders
of the mountains' northern slopes

spring premonitions
shudder of wild pony flank
the relative speed of this year's clouds
to those beyond

& those reflected in the water
between here & Ynys Môn
here & any other island

a sandwich on a map
& stones disposed
in bronze age rearrangements

we lived in such a settlement
we never knew where the names came from
we never found out where they went

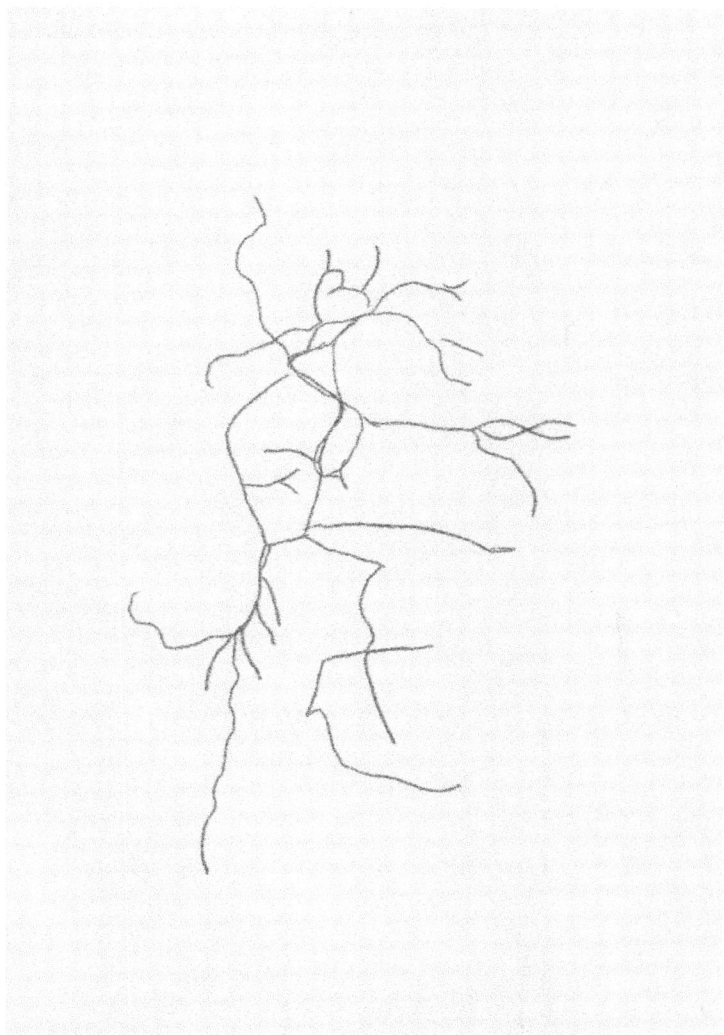

5

Carneddi – spring skylight
I wake up in a well
of moonlight

& lost voices
fractured seasons

resort to shadow play
& zig-zag tally marks
around the windows

down the road
the sea lifts its burdens
reflections of terror

& the flotsam
of the disappeared
the disappearing

6

rotate the drawing
through a quarter turn
each time

overlay shadows
from the same tree
throughout the day's
allocation of light

then 'sap moon' shades
birch sketch
      ash & holly
the ways the coming leaf
on every oak
can rearrange the song
of wind & alder
swept & drifted
willow charcoal
      light through
pewter water

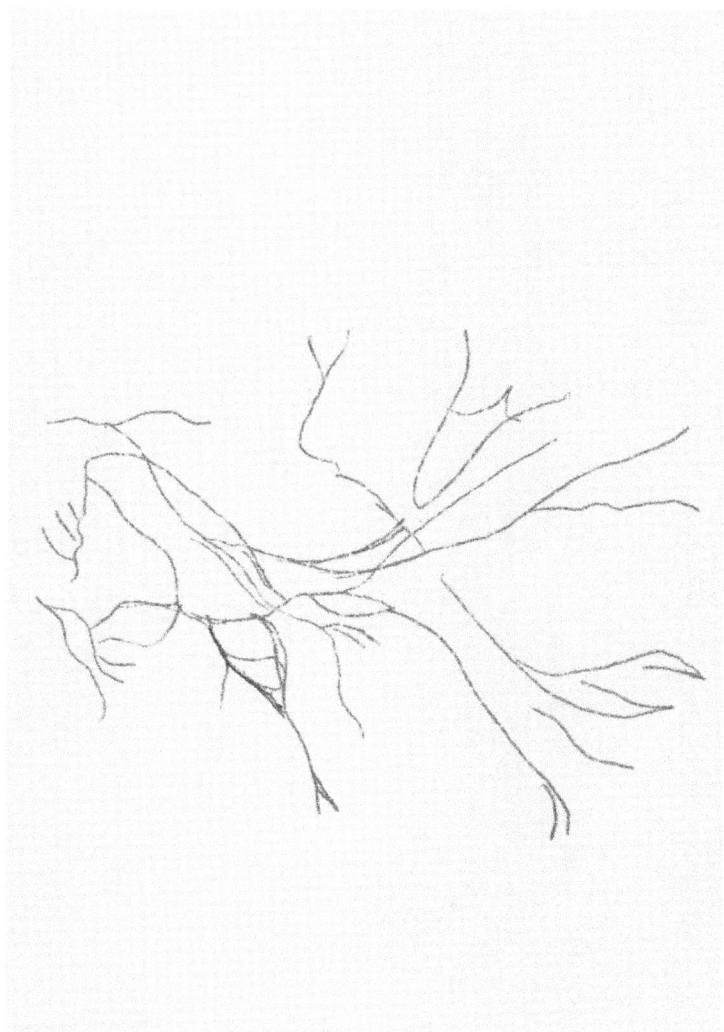

7

the drawings are not footholds
instructions or signs

or patterns for the knitting
which continues underground

abscission layer
leaf scar

the vascular bundles

wader tracks
back
to the ice cream van

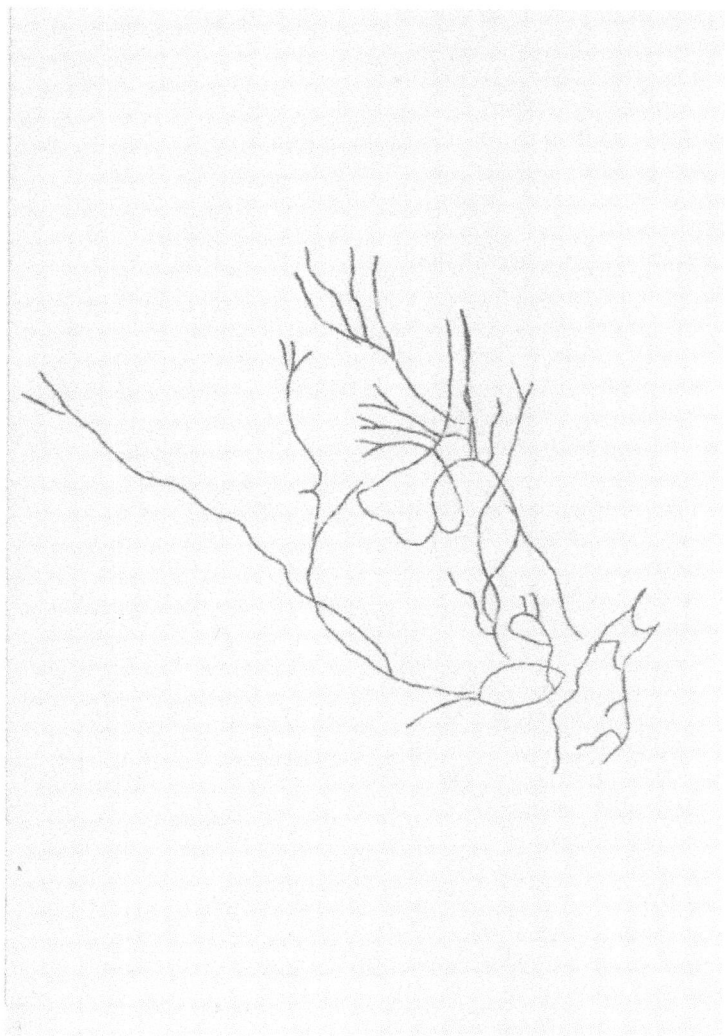

8

& small domed imprints
of brazil nuts in your icing

or the green lametta
tangled in her sports croc

or the dog toy Christmas pudding
lodged in the leylandii

see also apophatic

tiny insect tracks
between the grasses of the dunes

spellcheck inspiration
Lambeth
lament

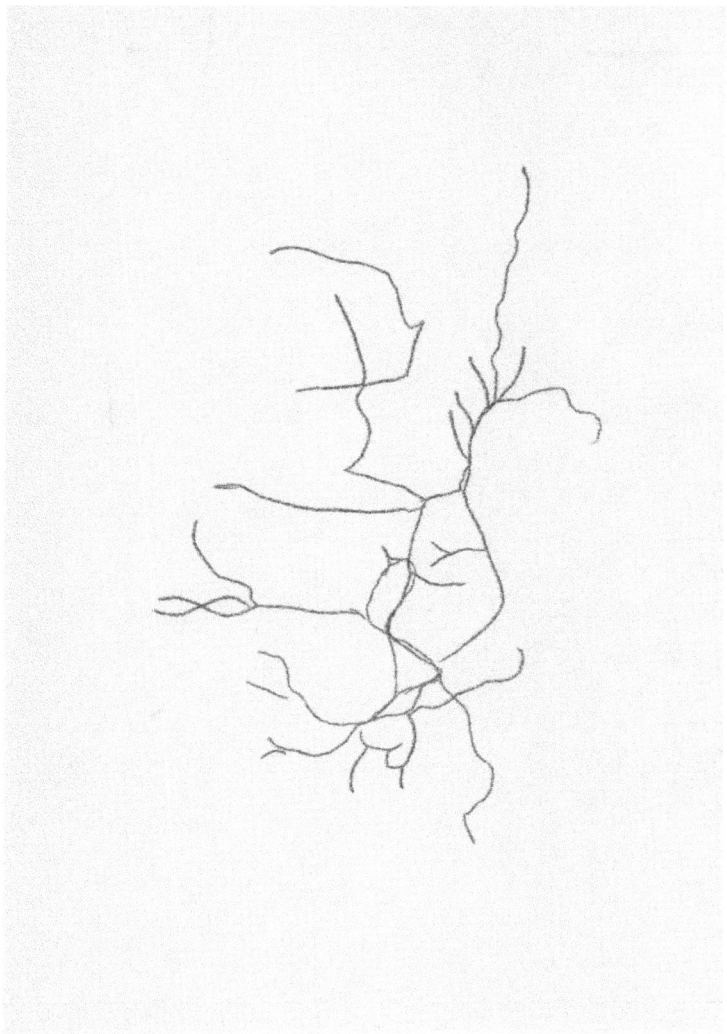

9

instead of starting with an outline

drag the side of broken
sticks of
charcoal

through the energy paths

then do something else

gardening
cooking
playing the instrument

taking circular walks
of increasing length
around your perch
or porch

OGWEN
for Lee

1

at the top of the valley
among the contributors
the River Ogwen is
neither here nor there
there isn't a beginning
you make a start
with where you are & what you've got
in your gut & blood
& on your mind
these glints cascading down
on every side from
one foot to another
short long short short long
the footholds still precarious
the dew not having
given up its light
a big stride up & onto
this flat rock then wait
until the dipper
makes its own way
further down
& then away into
the shadows
with not even a trace
of a thought as to

line selected up to now

wind from Ireland

bones & runes between the rocks

2

the river slings a load
of rubbish
around the bend
it's stuck
until the next
instalment of extreme
weather it's nuts
we say but good
for the allotment
a buggy in a tree
a dam of wrappers
fraying tarps &
1 tonne builder's bags
the willow pats your head
dog swept sideways down the chute
bounces out downstream
already set for section 3

3

no good sat there staring
at the river as it pulses on
massaging & extending
its locations
better to keep moving
even after death into
the greater play & mayhem
of light beyond the mouth

Giacomo da Lentini was a Sicilian poet who seems to have
written the very first sonnets. He was a notary at the the
court of Frederick II in Palermo in the early years of the 13th
century. Sicily in that period was already multicultural with
scholars, philosophers, scientists and artists from the Christian,
Judaic and Muslim traditions sharing thoughts and insights.
Giacomo absorbs and reworks the Occitan traditions and poetic
forms of southern France into local modes and procedures.
Interestingly there is no trace of his original Sicilian texts. We
have only the transcriptions into Tuscan. So translation and
adjustment, not to mention gentrification, in one way or another,
is there in his poetry from the start.

the magic lamp appears to work
warm breath & strokes translate me
while they tinker with the clock-hands
on the town's medieval tower
& harvest this year's olives from the sky

the genie swapped my spirit beast
for the pup of the pirate queen
the girl who set a course for dawn
then gently rearranged my mouth

☙

she's off to circumnavigate the island
& paint the way the wake unwinds
past shifting bays & headlands
see if she can find a new location
park that boat & come ashore

1

  chilies once plucked
from the bush
 hanging upside down
   from the beam in the kitchen ceiling
      by the woman in the cowgirl hat
        & little else
         are fucking wonderful

❦

  kennst du das Land
wo die Citroën
        veered off the highway
   into a valley of olives
     & vines inside my heart
       say six hours east
         of Carolina

2

it is 1225 in Palermo
the moonlight falling through December
theory & the window
won't be breaking anything but hearts
the Christmas lights are coming on
along the main streets & piazza

🐛

they say love grills a couple of hearts
on a single shish-kebab stick
but Jesus it feels so late in the day
& the moon is playing a *cor anglais*
through a small glass jar of tears
the kind they used to bury with the dead

3

            every continental philosopher
           was wondering how she could fit
                     through my eyes
   let alone be carted around in my heart
   I just sat down in Umbria
     one sunny late-May morning
        my back against an olive tree
             & something else took root

❧

       the pirate queen is checking her agenda
   running a salty forefinger haltingly down my chart
      butt dialling the harbour-master
    tending a pot of basil on the poop deck
in which my severed head is nurturing
    her aromatic leaves beneath the swaying stars

4

an unbelievably deep blue Advent
sky is chanting over Spello
& olive trees are doing those impressions
of transcendence
I still don't understand
which parts of me are functioning
it's hot and cold in different corners
of the terrace

❧

some of us are reading books
on post-traumatic stress
the left and right sides still not talking
as her sloop puts in to the dodgy
car-boot dockside of Palermo
everything goes everywhere

she paddles through blue shallows & reflections
with Puff Diddy – a new pet puffer fish
  who can't get the hang of swimming to heel
          or retrieving the pirate's tossed olives
        not that the Pirate Queen could give a damn
          as she exposes her wind-rose tattoo
        to the prevailing winds & constellations

❦

& remembers the Umbrian shadows
where *whisperedtoheldtightcaressed&fucked*
          became our temporary password
        nothing has ever been so easy to remember
      such Peruvian cuisine in sweet alignment
        with the personable music of her spheres
          & nights of Irish pipes & baccalà

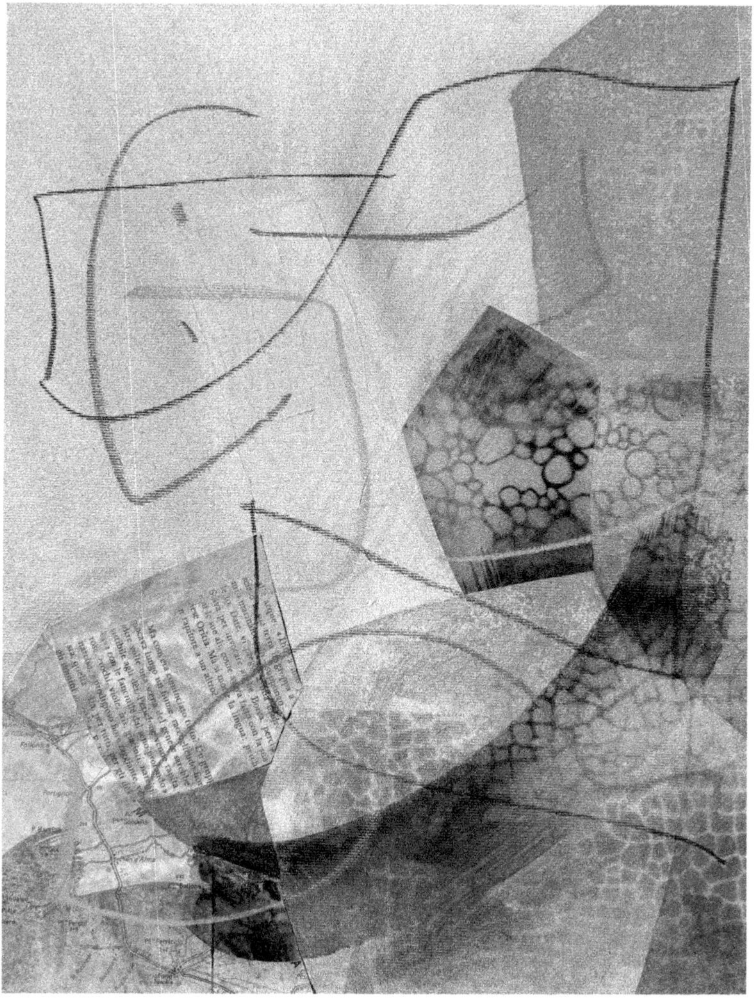

cowboy limps in
to the service station
one of the Droitwich
Earps perhaps
howdy
iawn
turns out
he's ridden in
from Rhyl
in search of coffee
& a whopper
we chew the fat
& wince on dregs
evaluate
the handles
on these pasties
attempting
to distinguish
yet again
between the hairy
and the buttery
we drawl farewells
at a matching pair
of rowdy
Dyson Airblades
& head back out
onto the trail
chewing on

Llangollen
juicy fruit
once more
& listening to
Neilson's 4th
The Inextinguishable
I hum along
negotiate the sheep
& think about
our European
days & mental
poverty & all
the people
without whom

as you rummage
for recalcitrant *vongole*
 in a brimming bowl
  the muffled underwater
   clicks & chatter
    of the clams
       add fresh percussive
         highlights & deflections
          to the deeper musics
            of the valley
              & the kitchen
                where a lean trio
                  of anchovies
                    & four fat cloves
                  of this year's garlic
                   embark upon
                  a new collaboration
                in the wide expanses
              of your aluminium pan
           whereas in itchy dreams
          concocted by mosquitoes
        & streams of vermentino
  I saw you stick
 a mini octopus
  on the front
   of your SG
   which served as
  temporary amp

& living strumbuddy
but also sang along
in wordless gurgling croons
such coy & plaintive tunes
as could be captured
by the engineers
at ECM
then blended with
the tread & lustre
of a battered old
acoustic bass
in timeless
Lombard airs

I'm whittling this
tascabile memorial
to Kenny Rogers
from a creosoted
sleeper I imagined
underneath the disused
slate-train track
that ran down
past Bethesda
to the harbour
with its brigs &
barques & schooners
plus a toy castle built
from slavery & sugar
country sorrow
in the West Indies
where early versions
of the blues
& catastrophic loss
ached & bled into
the American grain
& granary   it's a long way
from Bethesda down to
Georgia & Stradella
& the train I ride
stopped functioning
in 1962 then turned
into something else

let's call it travelling-time
as played on an acoustic
song without words
a set of blue-black
abstracts mostly
instrumental & the line
is now a cycle-track
where trees
meet overhead
& where we hum like cables
& finger different cords

the ash tree starts
remembering spears
& hears
new rumours
concerning human
dieback / reassembled covens
& leaders whose dunces caps
reach all the way down
to the forest floor
now that Beltane's past

       the edge of the plot
       is no longer the edge of the plot
       here at the redefined allotment
       with woven ash & hazel
       & a length of dry stone wall
       opposite an ugly
       stretch of chicken wire

I muse on separation
hilltop trysts
still echoing
through the season's
diminishing darkness
& blotched optics
the very big
looks like
the very small
bacteria & viruses
a deep space shot

from Hubble
  I read about preparing
    permanent slides
      for microscopy
        but end up deconstructing
          this dead washing machine
            its weights now anchoring
              the trampoline
                its drum

                        now full of fire

above the mountain
a mountain of bright
cumulus appears to
stretch but then forget
its absence of intentions
as wisps of is it
cirrus or just more
months of meandering
smokiness
begin to saunter
over the allotment
at about hip height
though not if you
are still sat down
as we do
be do so farewell then
Little Richard
& hello to this small nudge
among the waves
a darker smudge
becomes a small seal
of approval no
let's not be writing that
OK there's this much
of a sandwich left
then crumbs
an empty pack
of salty snacks

in Aberdaron
is this the face
that launched
a thousand crisps
another pair of oystercatchers
quoting Peter Riley
sea-pie sea-pie sea-pie
they don't say that
we'll make up something else

I had that dream again
the 4th saucepan
of the apocalypse
banging on the *caban* roof
with news of Goethe
teaming up with what's left
of the Stranglers
walking beaches
watching peaches
it's such a relief
to be following the tidelines
that curve around to
Llanddwyn Island
& thence into the sky
where I imagine Brahms
perusing Schoenberg's
early string quartet
before returning to the bay
& his own few final castles made of sand
how shall we spend the time that's left
maybe plant a little garlic
& toss these acorns into briars
where one or two may thrive
chop up another clump
of celery & onions
lob in a little mottled
pink snowman
head of frozen

turkey mince
turn down low
& open up another skin
of dark red wine
propose a toast
to all the eels
that swam in
Dwynwen's well

the clocks stumbled forward
months ago & I ignored them
masked & claustrophobic
while the unwashed sun glared out
on another season finale
of the clueless
driving up the rocky track
to the allotment
with a boot full
of 1950s Stermat tools
our elbows sticking out the window
we anticipate defrosted sausages
& listen to to a bit of early Brahms
in my dream I'd written
an ode to the burger van
on the Llandygai Industrial Estate
& won a lifetime's free supply
including the blackboard specials
the homemade Welsh lasagna
with its mesmerising densities
the piquant & succulent hug
of the chicken curry without chips
the Wednesday roast
the lamb-burger with its
mysterious accompaniment
the fulsome agglomerations
& pleasing etymology
of the Monday afternoon lob scouse

the Norwegian sailors'
second favourite
all set to music for alto & accordion
by Brahms who's sat there
murmuring German at the bus stop
waiting for his voice
to break

September breeze
in the Upstairs Wood
where sleek webs
trampoline & shimmer
in the oak & rowan
the juniper & birch
I don't know the name
of this butterfly
but the smooth bark
it's resting on is warm
my rock is covered
in a dense moss
afternoon heat full
the sun has half an hour
to go before it drops
behind the slate spoil
& after lunch
when I was dozing
a blue tit flew
into the cabin
& perched for
twenty seconds
on the lamp shade
staring at me as I
breathed in & out
we quietly watched
each other look
these things don't last long

now flat on my back under oaks
whose branches
strangely overlap
I think it may be
a Speckled Wood butterfly
neither of us is sure

the pier is closed for repairs
aren't we all
so we head for the hills & allotment
where two long-tailed tits
the only species of panda
native to Gwynedd
explore the inner mazes of the blackthorn
before returning to the nuts of Coed y Parc
who still work that neglected plot
replacing rotten fence posts
sharing out the donkey muck
pruning the afflicted ash
weeding the recalcitrant beds
or crossing out a couplet in the notebook
the doctor says the sax pads
will need a bit more dubbin
a robin wants to nest
in the stringless guitar
the trumpet has a rodent
sleeping in the bell
inspiring a gently modal tune
which may be called the Dormition
of the Dormouse *glis glis*
after its favourite skiing manoeuvre
the long-tailed tits are back in the hedge
they can't make their minds up either
we're all getting ready
& we're getting ready slowly

because you never know for certain
what it is you're going to need
or who you're going to ask
to hold the ladder

Marsh relaxing on the bridge
above the braided river
relishing the relative freshness
of air spritzed up by the Staffora
the sky irregularly spirals by
as does the river nonchalantly
pottering aware it will be back
to hear again this antiphon
by Hildegard von Bingen
the Sibyl of the Rhine
who fingered such a range of pies
& knew a lamprey from a lamppost
he remembers the expression
angels with horns
as well as the only true salami
to intrude upon his otherwise
pescatarian practices & creed
you wouldn't think that under heaven pigs
could emanate such rarified aromas
no hint of bog
ammonia or trough
& there is no time
like the birthday present
yes it's flawed & awkward
to savour angles & humidity
insubstantial imaginings
the lights & sounds & flavours
all located in the actual
four dimensions of the valley

behind the bar
there's suddenly this
mad festivity of fireworks
& the sky's alive with bats
   for nearly
as long as it takes to notice
   that they've gone
the ripples in the valley's
quiet bowl
die away into this glass
of still *grecchetto*
   on the terrace
by the citronella candles
   & star lounger
well now we wait
resisting sleep & pesky thoughts
though thinking will still glimmer
   around the edges
   it's often overrated
a long-awaited shooting star
   flicks the edge
   of Cassiopeia
& someone's wish in Collepino
way up beyond the other side of town
   the terrace looks out over the piazza
where streetlights shine till dawn
& the constant trickle of the fountain
murmurs on throughout the night

La magnamo o la 'ncartamo?

I'm stumbling through the veils of curdled light
etc   numb as they come   Mahler kazoo
 angels of the air are trembling into
        hallucinogenic existence again
            down the terraces & slopes of the Chiona
        with the woodland fungal fevers
        & the language malnutrition
     with the benzine vermentino
  with my harvest pouch of feral capers
 & my bitten ears still ringing to the hoots & jives of
Francesco & his Portative Organ
 plus the dissolution of the sound of every vowel
    the Troposphere jerkily dances being pecked to death
     by rabid guys who hide in language & bananas
        adverts & chat about Blake's death mask
         recall his final exclamation
        before he ducked behind the curtains
      to reappear as Dr Who – we're wondering
     is this a world that William Hartnell would've wanted?
 people also ask: are capers made of seaweed?
how long do capers last once they've been opened?
 do capers make good pets?
   do people still wear capers?
     are capers eligible for high office?
   how many capers could I fit in my arse?
        check in again next week in time to enter
        the amazing world of the anchovy

questo Trebbiano Spoletino
rolls off the tongue
& down the throat
as skyline pigeons
& the neighbours
peer over the shoulders
of the town & wonder
how to contemplate September
order firewood
air the winter coats
out on the terrace
observe the jostling grapes go trundling by
I book my teeth & eyes in for a service
try to coax my slothful summer
mind down from its tree
a mind now turning into amber
with attention spanlets shorter
than those of pickled capers
early stars look colder
later stars more distant
I'm getting notes of almond flower
acacia & finely-ground white pepper
I'm getting minerals / bruised peaches
on a breeze from Collepino
beneath this waning gibbous moon
I'm getting precipice

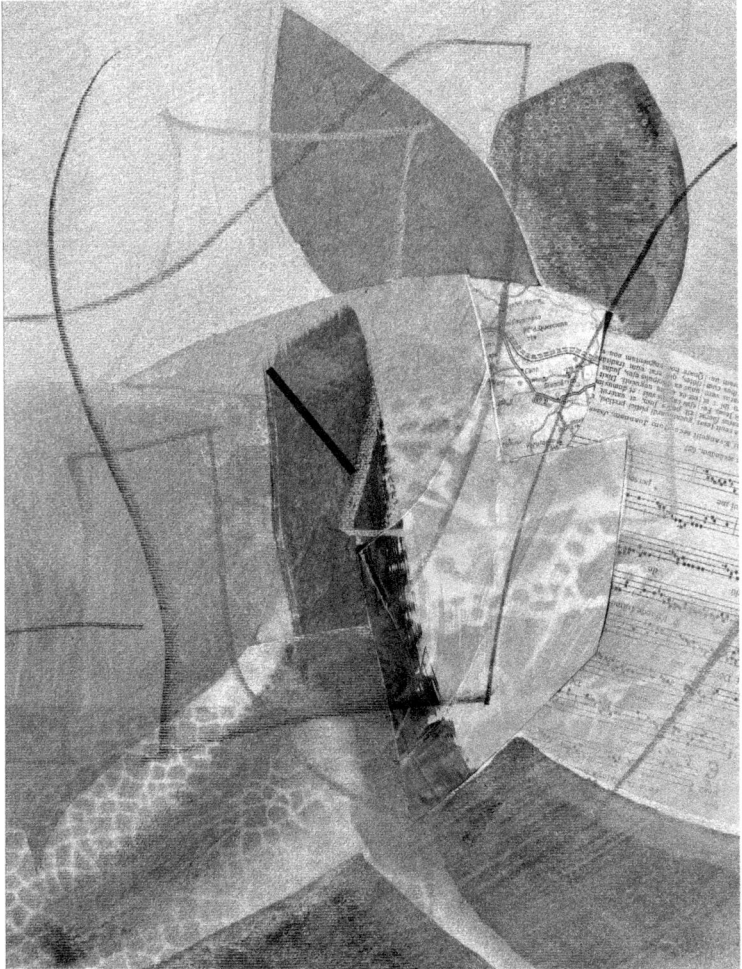

threading the upper & the lower worlds
a lizard nips behind the caper plant
that's rooted in the limestone wall
la lucertula protects the crops & children
relates to Bacchus & the vines
connects the Trebbiano
& Grecchetto from Cannara
overseeing these translations
& the clarinet quintet by Brahms
in Sant'Andrea of the shaded echoes
a coin dropped in a well
& a bubbling up into the melody
which springs & then accommodates
the ancient melancholia as light
might interleave its fingers
with those of night
the tree branch shadows
& a mild October wind
blows through the mind's
dishevelled & vacated nest
this glass is still half full
although they're clearing up in the piazza
they wipe away the crumbs & moonlight
briefly swims in dampness
as the tables dry

ACKNOWLEDGEMENTS

Some of these poems first appeared in 'Junction Box', 'Tentacular' and 'Noon: Journal of the Short Poem'. Many thanks to the editors.

'Let's Dantz' began as a collaboration with David Rees and the original sequence, complete with all seven of David's pictures, can be found on Junction Box at this address:

https://glasfrynproject.org.uk/w/6864/peter-hughes-and-david-rees-lets-dantz/

The complete Lentini versions appeared as 'Jack Lentini & the Pirate Queen' from KF&S.

The drawings which accompany the poem sequence 'Drawn' are Lisa Santana Hudson's *Llyn Padarn Glyphs*. Many thanks to Lisa for sharing them. Other images are by the author.

The 'Re:lode' poems are from an ongoing collaboration with Simon Marsh. He writes the odd ones, I do the evens.

Special thanks to Steve Xerri for his generous input on design.

LAY OUT YOUR UNREST